DK SUPER Planet
Global Gardens

Grow your knowledge of our world by exploring these glorious green spaces, from hot desert oases to icy Antarctic gardens

Produced for DK by
Editorial Just Content Limited
Design Studio Noel

Author Elizabeth Gilbert Bedia

Senior Editor Ankita Awasthi Tröger
Senior Art Editor Gilda Pacitti
Managing Editor Carine Tracanelli
Managing Art Editor Sarah Corcoran
Production Editor Jaypal Chauhan
DTP Designer Rohit Singh
Production Controller Rebecca Parton
Publisher Sarah Forbes
Managing Director, Learning Hilary Fine

First American Edition, 2025
Published in the United States by DK Publishing,
a division of Penguin Random House LLC
1745 Broadway, 20th Floor, New York, NY 10019

Copyright © 2025 Dorling Kindersley Limited
25 26 27 28 29 10 9 8 7 6 5 4 3 2 1
001–345408–Apr/2025

All rights reserved.
Without limiting the rights under the copyright reserved
above, no part of this publication may be reproduced, stored
in or introduced into a retrieval system, or transmitted, in any
form, or by any means (electronic, mechanical, photocopying,
recording, or otherwise), without the prior written permission
of the copyright owner.
Published in Great Britain by Dorling Kindersley Limited

A catalog record for this book
is available from the Library of Congress.
HC ISBN: 978-0-5939-6256-5
PB ISBN: 978-0-5939-6255-8

DK books are available at special discounts when purchased
in bulk for sales promotions, premiums, fund-raising,
or educational use.
For details, contact: DK Publishing Special Markets,
1745 Broadway, 20th Floor, New York, NY 10019
SpecialSales@dk.com

Printed and bound in China

www.dk.com

Contents

Glorious Gardens	4
An Indigenous Garden	6
An Icy Garden	8
A Towering Garden	10
A Deadly Garden	12
An Underground Garden	14
A Desert Garden	16
A Research Garden	18
An Underwater Garden	20
Space Gardens	22
Urban Gardens	24
Wild Gardens	26
Vertical Gardens	28
Bottle Gardens	30
Digging the Dirt	32
Everyday Science: Plants as Medicine	34
Everyday Science: Seed Banks	36
Let's Experiment! Growing Greens	38
Let's Experiment! Colorful Containers	40
Vocabulary Builder: Dr. Sanchez's Rainforest Log	42
Glossary	44
Index	46

Words in **bold** are explained in the glossary on page 44.

Glorious Gardens

The oldest gardens can be traced back thousands of years to when humans started to settle in one place. Now, gardens grow on every **continent** on Earth. They are found in every **climate**—from icy tundra to dry desert. Gardens are important **habitats** for wildlife. They provide animals with food and shelter. By reducing **pollution** and helping fight **climate change**, gardens are also important to the **environment**. They are also beautiful!

Trees provide us with clean air to breathe. Scientists estimate that some trees can support more than 2,300 wildlife species.

The painter Claude Monet was fascinated by nature. He often painted the water lilies in his garden in France.

Japanese-style gardens allow people to connect with nature. They are places of meditation and mindfulness. This garden is in Kyoto, Japan.

Even in subzero South Pole **temperatures**, there are gardens. In this indoor garden at China's Great Wall Station in Antarctica, scientists grow vegetables in greenhouses.

The Gardens by the Bay, in Singapore, are famous for their Supertrees. These giant structures are covered with more than 160,000 plants.

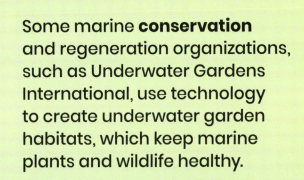

Some marine **conservation** and regeneration organizations, such as Underwater Gardens International, use technology to create underwater garden habitats, which keep marine plants and wildlife healthy.

An Indigenous Garden

Some gardens work to preserve indigenous plants and trees. These are the plants and animals **native** to that area. The Origins Center Indigenous Garden in South Africa grows many indigenous plants. It honors the Indigenous people who grew and used the plants as medicine, shelter, and food for centuries.

Aloe plants have many healing **properties**. Gel from their leaves can soothe burns and cuts.

Some plants stink! The African starfish plant smells like rotten meat. Its smell attracts flies that help **pollinate** it.

Fascinating fact

The spiky branches of acacia trees give protection to birds and their young from **predators**.

Habitats of Africa

Earth's continents contain many habitats, including desert, polar, and underwater habitats.

Africa is one of Earth's continents and is full of different habitats, from dry deserts to snowcapped mountains and lush rainforests (*above*).

Sedge grows along riverbanks. Birds build nests with it. Elephants and hippos eat it. Long ago, people used it to make sleeping mats.

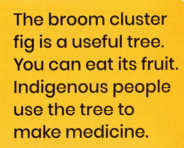

The broom cluster fig is a useful tree. You can eat its fruit. Indigenous people use the tree to make medicine.

Almost one-quarter of Africa is covered in forests that are home to many species of birds and animals. This Guinea turaco (*above*) lives in the rainforest and eats flowers and tropical fruit.

An Icy Garden

In Antarctica, penguins, seals, and whales hunt in exceptionally cold temperatures. The only things that grow outside here are **algae**, **fungi**, **lichens**, and **mosses**. Approximately 1,000 scientists and workers live in Antarctica all year round. They need a way to grow fruit and vegetables to eat. Their solution? Indoor gardens.

Antarctica is mostly covered by ice. In some places, scientists estimate the ice is almost 3 miles (4.8 km) deep.

Penguins, along with most other animals in Antarctica, eat tiny shrimp-like krill. Blue whales eat over 35,000 lb (16,000 kg) every day. Krill are decreasing due to rising **ocean** temperatures.

Antarctic mosses, lichens, and algae do not need roots to survive. They can absorb water and grow with little sunlight.

Mawson Station is an Australian research base in Antarctica. In the winter, only around 20 people live there. But in the summer, this number is over 50.

Fascinating fact

Mawson Station is in an area with some of the fiercest winds on the planet. Turbines use these winds to make electricity.

Gardens without soil?

At Mawson Station, people use hydroponic gardens to grow fruit and vegetables indoors.

A hydroponic garden is a type of indoor garden. Plants here grow in water, not soil. The water has **nutrients** to help the plants grow.

In a hydroponic garden, people can control the lighting, temperature, and **humidity** in the environment.

A Towering Garden

A gigantic rock formation towers over the tropical jungle in Sri Lanka, in Asia. This is Sigiriya. This was once the fortress of King Kashyapa. He built the gardens here over 1,500 years ago. They are some of the oldest gardens in the world.

The gardens are home to tropical fruits such as coconut, banana, guava, jackfruit, and mango (*above*).

Sigiriya means "lion's rock." Two giant lion paws carved out of the rock guard the entrance to the fortress.

Find out!

Can you find out how many steps you must climb to reach the top of Sigiriya?

About 1,200.

Sigiriya has trees that produce spices we use every day, such as cinnamon, nutmeg (*left*), and pepper.

Toque macaque monkeys are just one of the many animals that live in and around Sigiriya.

Little green bee-eaters are native to Sri Lanka. They eat wasps and other insects, as well as bees!

Reservoirs were built to catch rainwater during the wet season. Water flows to the different gardens through canals.

Asian elephants visit Sigiriya after the **monsoon**. Monsoons occur in tropical climates after the summer. They bring rainstorms that last for days.

A Deadly Garden

Gardens can be deadly. That is, if they contain poisonous plants. These are plants that can make you very sick if you touch or eat them. Many are quite rare, but some grow in our own backyards. The Poison Garden in Alnwick, England, is full of poisonous plants. Let's explore some of the plants you can find there.

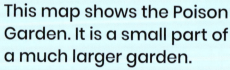

If touched, the gympie-gympie's leaves cause an allergic reaction. It feels like you are getting an electric shock.

This map shows the Poison Garden. It is a small part of a much larger garden.

All visitors have to wear protective clothing to enter the Poison Garden.

If eaten, deadly nightshade causes confusion, blurry vision, and death.

Find out!

Can you find out which deadly plant gets confused with wild parsnips and celery?

Water hemlock.

Poisonous plants for dinner?

Some animals can eat poisonous plants without getting sick.

Koalas eat eucalyptus, which is poisonous to humans. Their bodies can break down the poison, which makes the plant safe for them to eat.

Many deer eat plants that are poisonous to other animals, such as poison ivy and yew. They only eat small amounts so they do not get sick.

Rhododendrons are grown in many gardens because of their colorful flowers. But if eaten, they can cause an upset stomach.

An Underground Garden

Some gardens grow and flourish in **microclimates**, which exist all over the world. There are natural ones, like an oasis in a desert. There are also artificial ones, like a greenhouse in the tundra. An underground garden in California, in North America, is well-known for its microclimate.

The climate in central California is too dry to grow citrus trees. So, a man named Baldassare Forestiere built underground gardens.

Fascinating fact

It took Baldassare 40 years to build his underground garden. He did it with help from his two mules, Molly and Dolly.

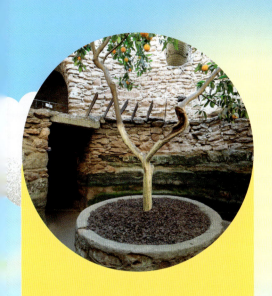

The temperature and humidity underground were perfect. Baldassare planted orange and other fruit trees. Large openings let light in.

Microclimates affect temperature, **precipitation**, and soil quality. They can also make the growing season longer or shorter. An oasis is one type of microclimate. It is cooler than the dry desert around it.

A cave is a microclimate. This is because the climate underground can be cooler and more humid than it is at Earth's surface.

Greenhouses are microclimates. They use **energy** from the Sun to create a warmer climate.

A Desert Garden

Even in the dry desert, you can find gardens, like the Alice Springs Desert Park in Australia. This garden really comes alive at night because many of the animals that live here are nocturnal. This means they are awake at night and asleep during the day.

Thorny devils only eat small black ants that nest underground. They can eat more than 1,000 ants at a time.

The desert park is inspired by the relationship between the plants, the wildlife, and the Indigenous people known as the Arrernte.

Fascinating fact

Traditional Arrernte healers are known as Angangkere. They use native plants as medicine to help people's health and wellbeing.

Nocturnal animals

It is wild in the desert at night. Predators hunt for food. Their **prey** hide in the plants and rocky landscape.

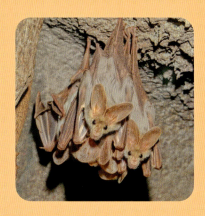

Bilbies are **marsupials** that are active at night. They eat insects, plant roots, seeds, and fruit. Bilbies burrow into the ground to hide from predators.

Ghost bats get their name from their light fur and **transparent** wings. They hunt at night for small mammals and reptiles.

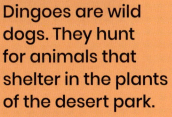

Dingoes are wild dogs. They hunt for animals that shelter in the plants of the desert park.

Bandy-bandies are nocturnal snakes. They have **adapted** to eat blind snakes, which are found across Australia. Bandy-bandies get their name from their stripes, which confuse predators and prey.

Echidnas are small mammals covered in spines. They mostly look for food at night. Along with platypuses, they are some of the only mammals on Earth that lay eggs!

A Research Garden

Many gardens in the world work to promote the conservation of plants and animals. They also aim to understand local **ecology**. They do this by carrying out research on plants. Ecology is the study of plants and animals in their environment. Conservation helps protect and preserve the plants and animals that are important to their environment.

The garden is a center of research and conservation of native plants and animals.

The Bogotá Botanical Garden in Colombia, South America, has a diverse **ecosystem**. It has dry forests and tropical rainforests.

There are about 19,000 plants in the garden. It has special collections of native plants that are at risk of going **extinct**, including some orchids and cacti.

Fascinating fact

The Bogotá Botanical Garden is the largest garden in Colombia!

Plants and animals of Colombia

Colombia is home to many plants and animals.

Unlike other palm trees, the wax palm thrives in cooler temperatures. At a maximum height of 196 ft (60 m), it is Earth's tallest palm.

The garden has six huge greenhouses. Each one has been designed to collect rainwater. Some are full of plants from tropical forests, one is dedicated to useful plants, and one is a **biodiversity** center.

Many native animals—such as toucans (*above*), parrots, lizards, and spiders—call Colombia's rainforests home. They help keep the plants healthy.

An Underwater Garden

Some gardens help keep our ocean ecosystems healthy. Underwater Gardens International is a marine conservation and regeneration organization in Spain. It uses technology such as three-dimensional (3D) printing to make habitats for ocean life. These habitats can be changed as conditions in the ocean—such as the temperature—change.

Fascinating fact

Underwater Gardens International is the first organization dedicated to restoring ocean ecosystems.

Scientists are hoping the 3D-printed habitats will help animals like corals. Corals are turning white and dying due to rising ocean temperatures and pollution.

Scientists use 3D printing to make habitats like reefs. They monitor the health of the habitat and make changes if needed.

People can dive to visit the gardens. Visitors can even help care for them.

The artificial reef habitats can help increase biodiversity. They also absorb harmful **greenhouse gases** from the environment.

Underwater Gardens International is working to open a park where people can learn about protecting ocean habitats.

Space Gardens

Some gardens are grown for our future. **Astronauts** on the International Space Station (ISS) are trying to grow gardens in space without sunlight or **gravity**. Astronauts hope these gardens will help future scientists understand how to grow fruit and vegetables on other planets.

The ISS has been home to astronauts from countries around the world since November 2000.

Find out!

Can you find out which vegetable astronauts first grew and ate in space?

Red lettuce.

Before going into space, scientists grow plants in the space station simulation center on Earth. It helps them understand how plants might grow in space.

On the ISS, plants grow in a special room called "Veggie."

Plants like lettuce and mustard are given water and nutrients. They get light that mimics sunlight and air that mimics the air on Earth.

Urban Gardens

In cities, **urban** gardens thrive among soaring skyscrapers, old railways, and even in airports. They can be as large as a city park, or as small as a few plants on someone's balcony. Urban gardens are good for the environment. They provide food to local people. They are also good for people's health.

The High Line in New York City was once an abandoned railway. The garden was designed to look wild, and contains a wide variety of native plants.

The University of Warsaw Library garden is a rooftop garden. It was designed so people could enjoy nature without leaving the city.

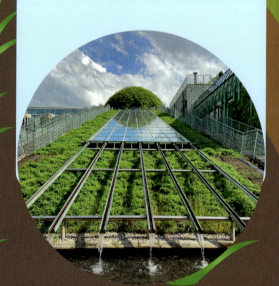

Find out!

Some of the earliest roof gardens were grown in ancient Mesopotamia. Can you find out the name of the buildings where they were grown?

Ziggurats.

Gotham Greens grows fresh produce in cities across the US. Their greenhouses use energy from the Sun and wind to make electricity.

Airport gardens

Some gardens can even be found in airports.

Changi Airport in Singapore is home to an amazing garden. A huge shopping center there hosts the world's tallest indoor waterfall, a garden maze, and lush green walkways.

Chicago O'Hare International Airport in the US is also home to an airport garden. It can grow over 1,100 plants at once. These plants grow vertically on 26 towers.

Wild Gardens

From the Arctic to the **equator**, there are gardens that grow wild. A wild garden is full of native plants. Native plants thrive in the climates that occur in their natural environment. Plants in the Arctic grow well in very cold conditions. And tropical plants grow well in their hot, wet habitat.

Black-eyed Susan *(right)* and yarrow *(left)* are native plants found across North America.

Fascinating fact

Native plants are usually far less affected by diseases and pests than **non-native** plants. This helps the ecosystem to thrive.

The Kirstenbosch National Botanical Garden is in South Africa. It is full of native plants from the country's different regions.

For centuries, Indigenous people have used native plants for healing. Many grow at Kirstenbosch, such as this paddle plant.

The Arctic-Alpine Botanic Garden in Norway is the world's northernmost botanical garden.

Native plants such as yellow poppies flourish in the cold climate and among the rocky landscape.

The imaginative gardens of Las Pozas are deep in the Mexican jungle, high in the mountains.

Here, native plants and trees grow wild among artificial stone sculptures and art.

Vertical Gardens

Gardens are not just good for their beauty. They can also help solve problems. In some cities, people are planting trees, shrubs, and flowers on the sides of buildings. These vertical gardens can help absorb harmful greenhouse gases in the environment, which makes the air cleaner. Greenhouse gases contribute to climate change.

It took seven years to build the Milan Vertical Forest. The two towers that form the forest contain as many plants as a natural forest that is 10 times as big.

Find out!

Can you find out the names of three different greenhouse gases?

Carbon dioxide, methane, nitrous oxide, and water vapor are some examples.

The Milan Vertical Forest is home to many plants. It is also home to 20 species of birds, such as blackbirds (*above*) and pale swifts. Harmful pests are eaten by insects like ladybugs.

L and TR Milan Vertical Forest designed by Boeri Studio. BR Wonderwoods designed by Stefano Boeri Architetti

Cars and factories produce harmful greenhouse gases. Vertical forests like the one in Milan take in carbon dioxide, which is a greenhouse gas. They use it to make oxygen. This helps fight climate change.

Vertical forests, like Wonderwoods in Utrecht, Netherlands, benefit communities. The plants make it easier to heat and cool buildings.

Bottle Gardens

Some gardens do not need to be watered. They can provide all the water they need by themselves. These amazing gardens are planted in glass containers called terrariums. Some terrariums are sealed containers, while others are open. If conditions are right, closed terrarium gardens create their own unique, self-sustaining ecosystems.

Fascinating fact

In the early 1800s, plants died on long sea voyages. Terrariums became a good way to transport living plants to new locations.

1 The plants take in energy from the Sun. As they take in energy, they give out water.

Closed terrariums can survive for a long time. One of the oldest known closed terrariums was planted in 1960. It was last watered in 1972 and has not been watered since!

2 The water can't leave the terrarium. It builds up on the container. Eventually, the water rains back down on the plants.

3 When the plants lose leaves, the leaves break down in the soil. This adds nutrients back into the soil.

4 These nutrients give the plants what they need to survive.

Open terrariums are good for growing desert plants like cacti. They do not need as much moisture as the plants in a closed terrarium do.

Digging the Dirt

Soil is important to the health of plants. Soil holds in water, which plants need to survive. It also holds important nutrients. As plants grow, they use up the nutrients in the soil. **Decomposers** return nutrients to the soil. This allows plants to continue to thrive. It keeps food chains and ecosystems running.

Find out!

The largest organism on Earth is a fungus. Can you find out what it is called and how big it is?

The Armillaria ostoyae covers 3.5 sq miles (more than 9 sq km).

You can find many decomposers in the soil of an ecosystem.

Decomposers such as earthworms break down dead plants and animals. Some only break down certain things, while other decomposers break down lots of different materials.

HOW DECOMPOSERS HELP ECOSYSTEMS

Decomposers keep ecosystems healthy and balanced. Without them, dead material like leaves would pile up. Decomposers break this decaying and dead material down. This returns the nutrients that plants need to the soil.

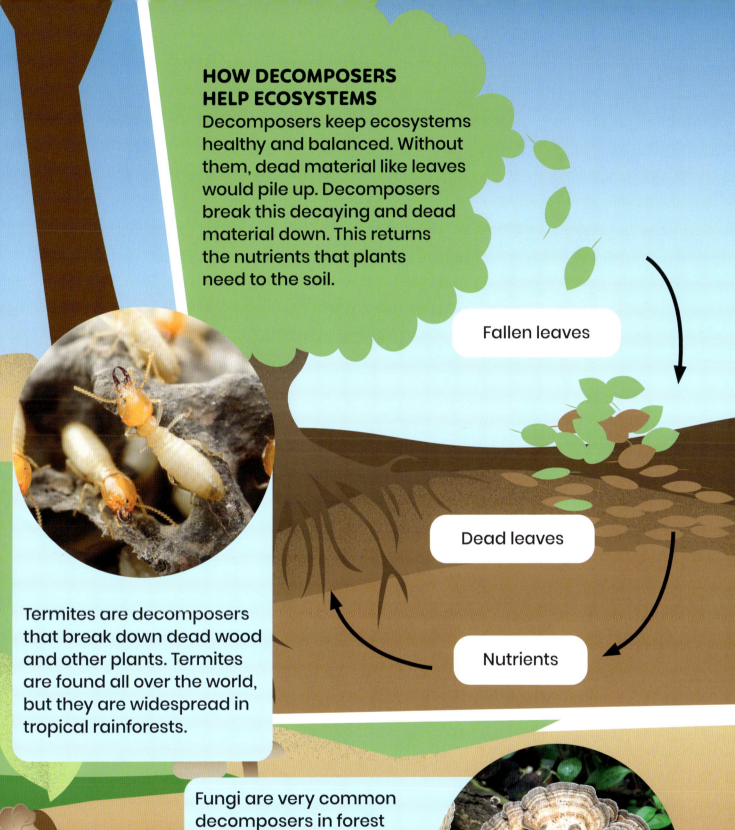

Fallen leaves

Dead leaves

Nutrients

Termites are decomposers that break down dead wood and other plants. Termites are found all over the world, but they are widespread in tropical rainforests.

Fungi are very common decomposers in forest ecosystems. They may look like plants, but they are not. They get all that they need to survive from dead plants and animals.

Everyday Science
Plants as Medicine

Many plants have healing properties. This means they can be used as medicine. Some of these healing plants grow in woodland such as conifer forests and tropical rainforests. Plants can also help people relax and feel good. They are good for our physical and mental health.

The thin, scaly bark of the Pacific yew makes medicine that is used to treat cancer.

Many mushrooms, including lion's mane and shiitake, are used for healing in traditional Chinese medicine.

Fascinating fact
Indigenous peoples in America have been using a huge variety of herbs in healing rituals for thousands of years.

The willow has been used to help with fever, swelling, and pain. A medicine similar to aspirin can be made from willow bark.

The importance of plants

Scientists are working to save native plants from the threat of **deforestation**. Deforestation destroys whole ecosystems, including the native plants found in them. When native plants are destroyed, we lose the chance to discover new medicines that could be made from them.

Being around plants can be medicine for our mental health. People can connect with nature and relax in forests.

Meditation gardens started in Japan. These are peaceful places where people can go to think, relax, and connect with nature.

Everyday Science
Seed Banks

Scientists store seeds in seed banks. These banks are used to preserve different plants from around the world. Seed banks also help maintain the world's food supply. Not just for now, but for thousands of years in the future. The Svalbard Global Seed Vault currently stores over 1 million seeds.

The fruit, vegetables, and grains we eat every day all started out as seeds.

The Seed Vault is in Svalbard, which is part of Norway. The vault was founded in 2008.

Canada

North Pole

Russia

Svalbard

Greenland

Finland

Sweden

Norway

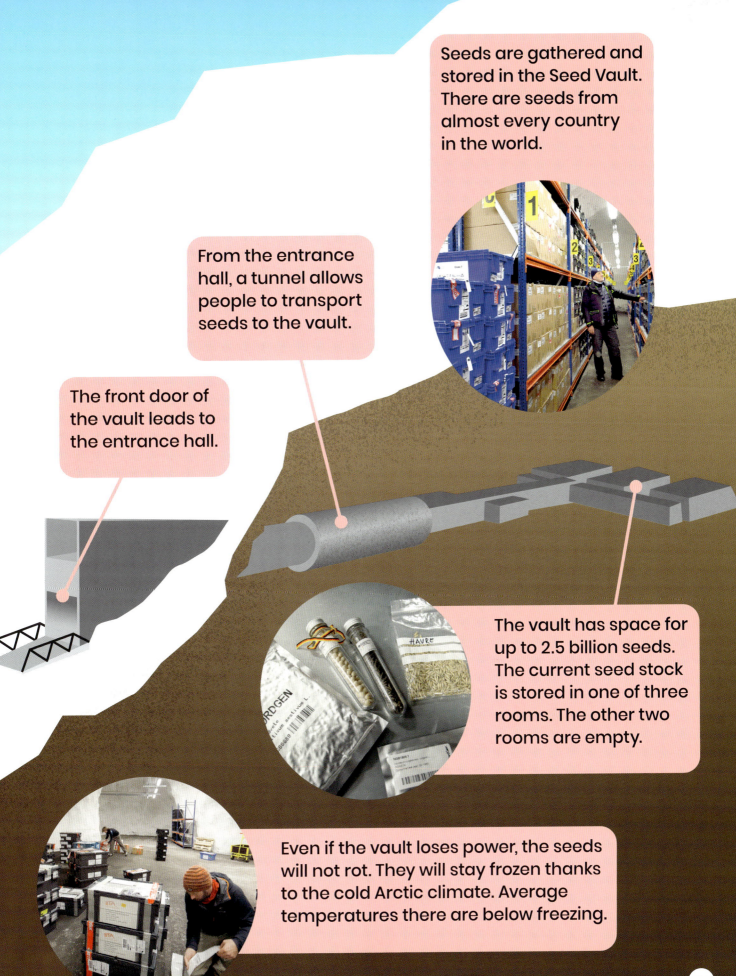

Let's Experiment!

Growing Greens

You do not need a garden to watch things grow! Build your own bottle garden to enjoy nature wherever you are.

You will need:
- A large plastic bottle
- String and scissors
- Cotton balls
- Three wooden skewers and modeling clay
- Seeds and water

Be careful when using scissors. Ask an adult to help you cut the plastic bottle and string.

1 Cut a large plastic bottle in half. Put the top half upside down in the bottom half. Pour in some water. The water should almost touch the top half of the bottle.

2 Cut five pieces of string. Put four through the bottle top. The ends should touch the water. Leave some string in the top half of the bottle.

3 Put cotton balls in the top half of the bottle. Put some seeds on top of the cotton balls.

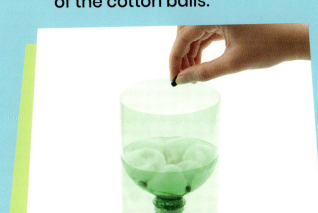

4 Now make a tripod plant support. Put a piece of modeling clay on the end of each skewer and tie them together with the last piece of string. Put the tripod in your planter. Watch your plants grow!

A HYDROPONIC VEGETABLE FARM

Hydroponic farming uses water and nutrients, instead of soil, to grow plants. Plants are grown indoors in special conditions. Artificial light takes the place of sunlight and the amount of water given to plants is controlled.

Let's Experiment!

Colorful Containers

Like all living things, flowers need water to survive. In this experiment, see what happens when flowers absorb colored water.

You will need:
- Three white flowers
- Three clear containers
- Scissors
- Water
- Food coloring (different colors)

Carefully cut the flowers or ask an adult to help you. Clean up any spilled water to avoid accidents.

1 Diagonally cut 0.8 in (2 cm) off the stems of the flowers.

2 Pour a small amount of water into each of the clear containers. Add some food coloring to each one. Use a different color each time.

3 Put a flower into each container. See what happens over the next few days!

A FLOWER MARKET

Scientists think that the very first flower on Earth had white petals. But today, flowers come in all kinds of different colors. Blue and purple are the rarest flower colors. The most common color varies depending on where you are. Some scientists think it might be green.

41

Vocabulary Builder
Dr. Sanchez's Rainforest Log

Scientists who study natural environments observe the plants and animals that live in those environments. They do this by carrying out fieldwork. This is work that takes place outside, not in an office. Read Dr. Sanchez's log of fieldwork in the rainforest.

Day 1: We made it to the rainforest. We are here to study this amazing habitat. How do the plants, animals, and organisms live in this environment?

Day 3: From our research base, we can see miles of green plants. The rainforest has a tropical climate. It is very hot and it rains a lot!

Day 14: So far, we have studied ten different plant and animal species. Our goal is to understand how the species interact in this ecosystem.

Day 19: We took some soil samples to study. We looked at the soil under a microscope. There were tons of bacteria and other tiny organisms.

Day 21: After three weeks here, we believe the ecosystem is stable. It has high biodiversity. And it is not under threat of deforestation. I wish we could stay longer!

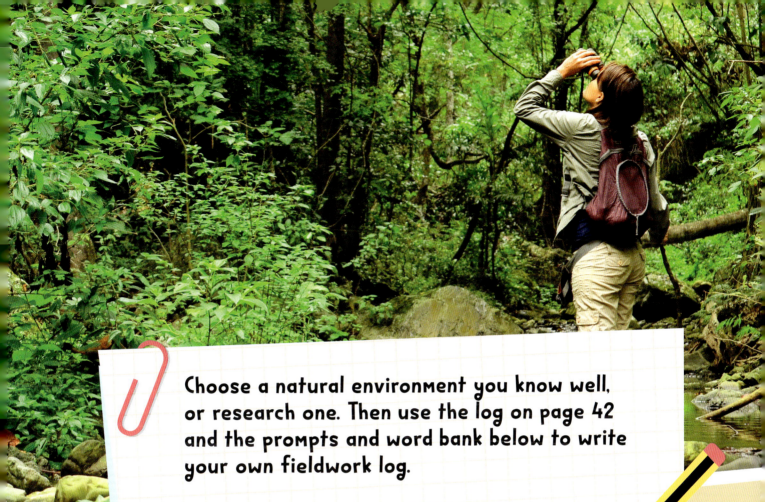

Choose a natural environment you know well, or research one. Then use the log on page 42 and the prompts and word bank below to write your own fieldwork log.

- What might you do and see there?
- What will you study?

What scientists do	carry out research	study
	do field work	test
	investigate	watch
	observe	work in a laboratory
	share research	write findings
What scientists study	animals	interactions
	biodiversity	organisms
	climate	plants
	ecosystems	relationships
	habitats	species

Glossary

Adapted Changed as a result of one's environment, in order to better survive.

Alga, algae A living thing found in fresh and salt water that makes its own food.

Astronaut Someone who works in space.

Biodiversity The variety of plant and animal species in a habitat.

Climate The prevailing weather conditions of a place over a long period of time.

Climate change The long-term changes in average temperature and weather patterns on Earth.

Conservation Preserving and protecting Earth's natural resources, especially plant and animal species and their habitats.

Continent One of Earth's seven landmasses—Antarctica, Africa, Asia, Australia, Europe, North America, and South America.

Decomposer A living thing that breaks down dead plants or animals and recycles these nutrients back into the soil.

Deforestation The act of cutting down forest so the land can be used for agriculture or manufacturing.

Ecology The study of living things and how they interact with their environment.

Ecosystem A community of living things that interact with non-living things in their environment.

Energy The ability to make things happen and cause changes.

Environment The place where a plant or animal lives and the interactions it has with the living and non-living things there.

Equator The imaginary line that circles Earth halfway between the North and South Poles.

Extinct Died out, such as a plant or animal.

Fungus, fungi A living thing that is found in soil or water.

Gravity An invisible force that pulls all objects down.

Greenhouse gas A gas in Earth's atmosphere that traps heat and contributes to climate change.

Habitat An environment where plants, animals, and other organisms live.

Humidity The amount of water in the air.

Lichen A living thing made up of algae and fungi that grow together on rocks or trees.

Marsupial A type of mammal that carries its young in a pouch.

Microclimate A small area where the climate is different from the climate that surrounds it.

Monsoon Extremely windy weather that causes very wet summers and dry winters.

Moss A plant without roots that grows in wet habitats as well as on rocks, tree bark, and so on.

Native Indigenous to an area.

Non-native Not indigenous to an area.

Nutrient A substance that helps plants and animals survive and grow.

Ocean One of the five main bodies of salt water on Earth.

Pollinate To take pollen from one plant to another, helping the plant make new seeds.

Pollution The process of releasing harmful things into the environment.

Precipitation Any liquid or frozen water that falls from the sky to the ground.

Predator An animal that hunts and eats other animals.

Prey An animal that is hunted by predators.

Property A quality that something has, such as its color, shape, or size.

Reservoir An artificial lake formed behind a dam that stores water.

Temperature How hot or cold something is.

Transparent See-through.

Urban To do with a city or town—an urban area is built up and many people live there.

Index

A
acacia trees 7
airport gardens 25
Africa 6–7
Alice Springs Desert Park 16–17
aloe plants 6
Antarctica 5, 8–9
Arctic 26–27
Arctic-Alpine Botanic Garden 27
Arrernte people 16

B
bandy-bandies 17
bilbies 17
Bogotá Botanical Garden 18–19
bottle gardens 30–31
broom cluster fig 7

C
caves 15
Changi Airport 25
Chicago O'Hare International Airport 25
climate change 4, 28, 29
Colombia 18–19
colorful containers experiment 40–41

D
deadly gardens 12–13
deadly nightshade 12
decomposers 32–33
deer 13
deforestation 35
desert gardens 16–17
dingoes 17
dirt 32–33

E
earthworms 32
echidnas 17
ecology 18
elephants 11
eucalyptus 13
experiments
    bottle gardens 38–39
    colorful containers 40–41

F
Forestiere, Baldassare 14–15
fungi 8, 32, 33

G
Gardens by the Bay 5
ghost bats 17
glorious gardens 4–5
Gotham Greens 25

gravity 22
Great Wall Station 5
greenhouse gases 21, 28, 29
greenhouses 5, 15
    Bogotá Botanical Garden 19
    Gotham Greens 25
Guinea turaco 7
gympie-gympie 12

H
habitats 4, 7, 20–21
High Line 24
hydroponic gardens 9, 39

I
icy gardens 8–9
indigenous gardens 6–7
Indigenous people
    American 35
    Australia 16
    South Africa 6, 7, 27
indoor gardens 5, 8, 9
International Space Station (ISS) 22–23

J
Japanese gardens 4, 35

K
Kirstenbosch National Botanical Garden 27
koalas 13

L
Las Pozas 27
little green bee-eaters 11

M
Mawson Station 9
medicine 6–7, 16, 34–35
meditation gardens 35
microclimates 14, 15
Milan Vertical Forest 28–29
Monet, Claude 4
monsoons 11
mushrooms 34

N
native plants 18, 19, 25–26
nocturnal animals 17

O
Origins Center Indigenous Garden 4

P
Pacific yew 35
palms, wax 19
penguins 8
Poison Garden 12

R
rainforest log 42–43
research gardens 18–19
reservoirs 11
rhododendrons 13

S
science
    medicine 34–35
    seed banks 36–37
sedge 7
seed banks 36–37
Sigiriya 10–11
soil 32–33
space gardens 22–23
starfish plant 6
Svalbard Global Seed Vault 36–37

T
termites 33
terrariums 30–31
thorny devils 16
toque macaque monkeys 11
toucans 19
towering gardens 10–11
trees 4

U
underground gardens 14–15
underwater gardens 20–21
Underwater Gardens International 5, 20, 21
University of Warsaw Library garden 24
urban gardens 24–25

V
vertical gardens 28–29

W
wax palm 19
wild gardens 26–27
willow 34
Wonderwoods 29

Acknowledgments

The publisher would like to thank the following for their kind permission to reproduce their photographs:

(Key: a-above; b-below/bottom; c-center; f-far; l-left; r-right; t-top)

123RF.com: Iurii Buriak 15tr, Mr.Smith Chetanachan 33cla; **Alamy Stock Photo:** Aeoliak 27bl, 27br, Alpha Stock 14cr, 15tl, Georgette Apol 20bl, Arctic Photo 27cl, Arterra Picture Library / Clement Philippe 32br, Botanikfoto / Steffen Hauser 12br, Christopher Doherty 21cr, DPA Picture Alliance 9cra, Randy Duchaine 25clb, Emilio Ereza 26bl, Jeffrey Isaac Greenberg 4+ 18tr, Michael Greenfelder 20cra, Hemis / Rieger Bertrand 37cra, Imaginechina-Tuchong 5cr, Incamerastock / ICP 5bl, Independent Photo Agency Srl Wonderwoods Vertical Forest projected by Stefano Boeri Architetti / Boeri Studio 29br, Maris Kurme 11tl, Richard Levine 9crb, M.Sobreira 27tr, Stuart McGowan 35cb, Ellen McKnight 24clb, NASA / Piemags 23tr, NASA Photo 23cla, Nature Picture Library / Jurgen Freund 17ca, Nature Picture Library / Kim Taylor 26tr, Nature Picture Library / Pal Hermansen 37bl, NTB / Heiko Junge 37cb, Papilio / Robert Gill 11tr, Picturelibrary 25crb, Francesco Puntiroli 19crb, Morley Read 35tr, Frederic Reglain 10clb, Science History Images 23br, Kumar Sriskandan 33br, Daniel Steeves 19cra, Zoonar / Carmen Mair 27cr; **Boeri Studio:** Wonderwoods Vertical Forest projected by Stefano Boeri Architetti 29br; **Depositphotos Inc:** Farina6000 36cra; **Dreamstime.com:** Christopher Bellette 16-17, Bilderbastler 8clb, Robero Dani 17cra, Ecophoto 27tl, Filedimage 16-17bc, Ken Griffiths 17cb, Jeep2499 13cra, Johannaralph 16tr, Juliasha 21bc, Nasir Alam Khan 7bl, Svitlana Kolchyk 24br, Kyslynskyy 11br, Magryt 31br, Max5128 10tr, Larry Metayer 12-13bc, Minacarson 41br, Nadin333 26br, Sean Pavone 35crb, Artinun Prekmoung 25tr, Ondřej Prosick 7crb, Just_Regress 39br, Roberto Ruggieri 5tl, Massimo Santi 4clb, Arkadij Schell 6cra, Peter Shaw 11clb, Sripfoto 32bl, Ssphoto 13crb, Staphy 8tr, Suburbanium 6bl, Swallace5 17crb, Sergey Uryadnikov 11cr, Vampy1 Stefano Boeri / S. Boeri, G. Barreca, G. La Varra 29tr, Veronika Viskova 15br, Yolfran 4tr, Zavgsg 21cla, Znm 7cra; **Getty Images:** Rosemary Calvert 8br; **Getty Images / iStock:** SeanPavonePhoto 4br, Trabantos 15cr; **Shutterstock.com:** AlvaroGO 43t, A. Blanke 10-11, GMY Timezone 12tr, Sarawut Konganantdech 7cla, MatthieuCattin 18cb, 19cl, R.M. Nunes Stefano Boeri / Milan Vertical Forest projected by Boeri Studio 28-29, Qnula 31tr, Taviphoto 28crb; **S. Boeri, G. Barreca, G. La Varra:** Stefano Boeri 28-29, 29tr

Cover images: *Front:* **Shutterstock.com:** andin76 c, Elena Istomina bl, My-Sun-Shine; *Back:* **123RF.com:** Iurii Buriak bl; **Alamy Stock Photo:** Aeoliak tl; **Dreamstime.com:** Svitlana Kolchyk cl

VOCABULARY BUILDER

THE NORSE GODS OF ASGARD

The pagan Viking gods live in the heavenly realm of Asgard. Asgard connects to other realms by a bridge called the Bifrost. Read these descriptions of the Norse gods of Asgard.

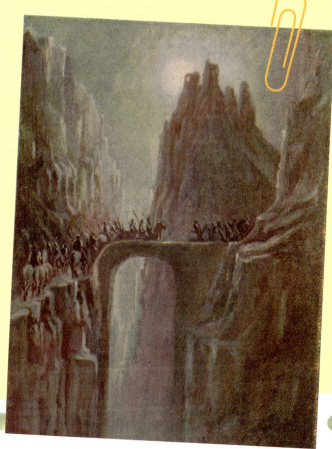

Odin
The one-eyed king of the gods and the god of war, wisdom, and magic is also known as the All-Father. Odin's companions are two ravens, Hugin and Mugin, and two wolves, Geri and Freki.

Frigg
Queen of Asgard and goddess of fertility and children, Frigg is brave and wise, and has the power to see the future.

Thor
Thor is the son of Odin and god of thunder and war. He is strong, good, and easily angered. He controls storms and protects humanity with his magic hammer, Mjöllnir.

Baldur
God of light and forgiveness, Baldur is Odin and Frigg's son. He is fair, beautiful, and kind. He is immune to disease, and the only thing that can defeat him is... mistletoe!

Loki
This shapeshifting trickster god was actually born a *jötunn* (giant) but became the adopted brother of Odin. He loves to make plots and sow chaos, but he's also silly and playful.

Freya
Goddess of love and beauty, Freya is caring and gentle. She makes prophecies and rides a chariot pulled by two huge cats, Bygul and Trjegul.

How are the gods described?
angry, beautiful, brave, caring, fair, gentle, good, kind, playful, silly, strong, wise

What are they gods of?
beauty, children, family, fertility, forgiveness, light, love, thunder, tricks, war, wisdom

Special powers or items
cat, chariot-riding, controlling storms, hammer, immunity, magic, prophecies, raven, seeing the future, shapeshifting, wolf

Create your own Norse god or goddess. Give them a name and write a description using the vocabulary boxes to help you.
- What special abilities do they have?
- What special items do they use?
- What do they look like?
- What is their personality?

GLOSSARY

Agriculture The practice of farming.

Alpine tundra Cold areas at high elevation, such as on mountains, that have few trees and plants because the ground beneath the soil is permanently frozen.

Archipelago A group or chain of islands.

Atmospheric gases The gases in the Earth's atmosphere, such as oxygen, nitrogen, argon, and carbon dioxide.

Biodiversity Variety in plant and animal life.

Boreal forest A forest that grows in northern regions where temperatures are below freezing for at least half the year.

Clean energy Energy that does not produce a lot of carbon dioxide.

Colonization The act of taking control of a land and settling by force, often displacing people who already exist there.

Congress A formal political meeting.

Conservation The preservation and protection of animals, habitats, and ecosystems.

Constitution A document that sets out the laws, beliefs, and rules for a country.

Crustacean An aquatic creature without a spine that usually has a hard shell, such as a lobster or shrimp.

Democracy A form of government in which the people in power are elected by the general population.

Ecological Relating to the environment and ecosystems.

Ecosystem A community of plants, animals, and other environmental factors that exist together with relationships and interactions that affect each other.

Elected government A government who was voted in by the people.

Fermented A chemical process applied to food and drinks that breaks down certain substances. It can be used to improve flavor and preserve food.

Glacier A huge mass of slow-moving ice.

Gulf Stream A stream of warm water that flows from the Gulf of Mexico.

Hydropower A form of renewable energy generated by water.

Ice age A long period of cold temperatures, in which glaciers cover much of the land.

Indigenous People whose ancestors were the earliest inhabitants of a land or those who inhabited a land before colonists arrived.

Inhabit To live in or occupy a particular place or area.

Invasive species A species that is non-native to an area but that has been introduced to and colonized that area. They are usually harmful to their environments.

Migrate Move from one place to another. For animals, this is usually done in groups and timed with seasons.

Mountain range A group or chain of mountains, usually with a name.

Norse Related to Scandinavia in the past, often the Viking era and before.

Omnivores Animals that eat both meat and vegetation.

Pagan Religious belief in nature and a set of multiple gods. Historically, this was often used to mean non-Christian.

Particle A tiny fragment, such as a molecule.

Polar Relating to regions around the North or South Pole.

Predator An animal that hunts and preys on other animals.

Public health system Healthcare that is available to everyone for free or for small fees.

Renewable energy Energy from a natural source that won't run out. This includes solar power, hydropower, and wind power.

Standard of living How comfortably people can live. It is measured by wealth and access to things like education, electricity, clean water, and suitable housing.

Subspecies A branch of a main species that is slightly different to the main species. For example, tiger is a species, and Bengal tiger is a subspecies.

Sustainable Affects an environment in such a way that the natural areas and resources can exist in future generations.

Tundra Cold areas with few trees and plants because the ground beneath the soil is permanently frozen.

Urban Related to towns or cities.

INDEX

A
allemannsretten 21
animism 23
archipelago 7, 44
Arctic Circle 7, 8, 17
Arctic foxes 12, 17, 23
Asgard 20, 42, 43
Aurora Borealis 7, 23

B
Bergen 4, 30
biodiversity 16, 44
"book town" 11
boreal forests 8, 9, 16, 31, 44
brødskiver 34
brunost 26, 34
bunad 6, 19, 24

C
carbon absorption 9, 16
celebrations 24–25
Christianity 22, 23, 24, 25, 37
Christmas 24, 27
climate change 15, 17
clothing, national 6, 19, 24
cloudberries 16, 27
coasts 9, 14, 15, 26, 30
colonization 37, 44
community 18
Constitution Day 19, 24
coral reefs 9
culture 18–21
customs 19

D
Denmark 4, 37
drinks 27

E
education 18, 31
employment 31
eplemost 27
exports 31

F
fauna 12–17
fermenting 26, 27, 44
festivals 24, 25
Finland 19
finnbiff 27
Fjærland 11
fjords 8, 9, 10–11
Flåm 11
flora 12, 16
folktales 20
food 11, 16, 26–29
forests 8, 9, 16, 31
Freya 43
Frigg 20, 37, 42

G
gákti 6, 19, 24
Galdhøpiggen 8
Germany 37
glaciers 11, 21, 44
Global Seed Vault 7
global warming 12, 17
gods and goddesses 20, 22, 23, 37, 42–43
government 37
Gulf Stream 9, 44

H
habitat loss 17
Harald I, Fairhair 37
Harald III, Hardrada 37
history 36–37
houses 30
hunting 17, 23
hydropower 6, 11, 31, 44, 45

I
ice age 11, 44
independence 37
Indigenous people 19, 44
 see also Sámi people
industries 31
invasive species 17, 45
Iron Age 36
islands 7, 9, 13, 15

J
Janteloven 18
Jostedalsbreen 11
jötnar 20
Jotunheimen 5, 20
julebrus 27

K
kelp 16
killer whales 15
kos 21
kraken 20
krumkake 27

L
lemmings 12, 13
lobsters 14

M
Margaret I, Queen 37
midnight Sun 7
Midsummer 25
monarchy 37
mountains 8, 21, 45
multekrem 27
myths 20

N
narwhals 15
national park 5, 20
noiade 23
Nordkapp 4, 5
Norse gods 20, 22, 37, 42–43
Norse people 36, 37
Northern Lights 7, 23
Norway spruce 16

O
Odin 20, 37, 42
Olaf II (St Olaf) 25, 37
Oslo 4, 6, 30

P
paganism 22, 25, 37
peiskos 21
pickling 26, 27
pink salmon 17
polar bears 7, 15, 17, 35
polar night 7
pollution 17
public health system 31, 45
public holidays 24
puffins 14, 17

R
rakfisk 26
raspeballer 26, 28–29
reindeer 9, 13, 19, 23, 27, 36
religion 22–23, 24, 25
renewable energy 31, 44, 45
ringed seals 15, 17
rivers 11, 17
rock ptarmigans 13
Russia 19
rutabaga 28

S
Saint Lucy's Day 25
Saint Olaf's Day 25
Sámi people 6, 8, 19, 23, 24, 36, 37
Sápmi 19
schools 31
sea eagle 14
smørbrød 26
Sognefjorden 10–11
sports 21
standard of living 18, 45
Stiklestad 25
subarctic 7, 8, 12
sursild 27
Svalbard 4, 7, 13, 15
Sweden 4, 19, 37

T
Thor 20, 37, 42
trolls 10, 20, 38
Trolltunga 20
tundra 8, 13, 16, 44, 45

V
Valhalla 43
Vikings 18, 36, 37, 42

W
walruses 15, 17
waterfalls 10
white-tailed eagle 14

Y
yoik 19

ACKNOWLEDGMENTS

The publisher would like to thank the following for their kind permission to reproduce their photographs:

(Key: a-above; b-below/bottom; c-centre; f-far; l-left; r-right; t-top)

Adobe Stock: Kushnirov Avraham 22, Sergey Bogomyako 9tr, marysckin 27clb, Lin V 24t, william87 37br; **Alamy Stock Photo:** James Berry 37tr, Chronicle 42tr, NTB 25cl, World History Archive 37cr; **Dreamstime.com:** Ab2147272 27tl, Ernest Akayeu 20tr, 28-29b (vegetables), 42-43 (Norse gods), F Baarssen 9cl, Natalia Chernyshova 7clb, Dmitry Chulov 11cla, Everst 21t, Frank Fichtmueller 13tl, Peter Hermes Furian 4cl, 4b, Boris Gavran 8, Aleksei Gorodenkov 31tl, Menno Van Der Haven 36, Jiri Hera 29bc, Andrei Hrabun 25bl, Oleksandra Klestova 33bc, Tetiana Kozachok 32-33 (Stationery), Dalia Kvedaraite 14b, Tomas Marek 11clb, Merfin 31ca, Igor Mojzes 21bl, Alexander Mychko 27cla, Nanisimova 10, Oksanabratanova 27bl, Roxxanna1 16tl, Vladimir Seliverstov 17tl, Shaiith 26t, Alexander Shalamov 21cl, Shapicingvar 6, Natalia Sokko 16cl, Oleksandr Sutchenko 31crb (x3), Adrian Szatewicz 9br, Stefano Zaccaria 30; **Getty Images:** The Image Bank Unreleased / Michel Setboun 23t; **Shutterstock.com:** Shpadaruk Aleksei 35r, Valda Butterworth 14tr, dreakrawi 19t, Ron Ellis 10b, everst 18, Andrey_Fokin 30b, Petros Goulas 25tl, GrumJum 28crb, Jan_Kuchar_Photo 16bl, Lyudmyla Kharlamova 28-29 (paper), 32tr, Lauritta 24b, lazydog20 7cl, Roland Magnusson 19cl, Borodacheva Marina 32-33 (Background), 34-35 (Background), Joe McDonald 15tl, Elizaveta Melentyeva 5, Muhammadphotoes 15cl, Hisa_Nishiya 32b, Konstantin Novikov 17tr, Nsit 28tr, Maciej Olszewski 14tl, Sofiia Popovych 34cb, Pro Symbols 26br, railway fx 6l, Risto Raunio 17b, Pavlo S 4br, See U in History 37cra, Simon's passion 4 Travel 23cl, SofieLion 12, Bjorn H Stuedal 13tr, Surajkalangada 26bl, David Pineda Svenske 20cl, Frederik Tellerup 19bl, Thx4Stock team 31clb (x2), TRphotos 7t, Tupungato 20br, urfin 29bl (cl), Sergey Uryadnikov 15bl, V. Belov 37crb, v.iraa 34-35 (Stickers), Karen Yomalli 13b

Cover images: *front:* **Getty Images:** Mike Hill br; **Getty Images / iStock:** lightpix cr, Nirut Punshiri t/ (Background); **Shutterstock.com:** alaver bl; *Back:* **Adobe Stock:** Sergey Bogomyako tl, william87 bl; **Shutterstock.com:** SofieLion cl

All of the books in the *Super World* series have been reviewed by authenticity readers of the cultures represented to make sure they are culturally accurate.